THE FOUR SEASONS

JAPANESE HAIKU
WRITTEN BY
BASHO · BUSON
ISSA · SHIKI · AND
MANY OTHERS

TRANSLATION BY
PETER BEILENSON

THE PETER
PAUPER PRESS
MOUNT VERNON · NEW YORK

A NOTE ON JAPANESE HAIKU

THE HAIKU is a seventeen-syllable poetic form that has been written in Japan for three hundred years. It has been enormously popular without becoming banal. For the *haiku* does not make a complete poem in our usual sense; it is a lightly-sketched picture the reader is expected to fill in from his own memories. Often there are two pictures, and the reader is expected to respond with heightened awareness of the mystical relationship between non-related subjects.

This mystical awareness is one of the seekings of Zen Buddhism, and was introduced into *haiku* by the first, best-loved, greatest master of the form, Basho (1644–1694). A second master was Buson (1715–1783), a poet less interested in mystical relationships than in exquisite vignettes. A third was Issa (1763–1827), pathetic, wryly humorous, utterly individual. A fourth was Shiki (1866–1902) — a modern Buson who gives us perfectly-phrased glimpses of everyday scenes and situations.

Almost every *haiku* holds a season key-word; often the name of the season itself, otherwise a seasonal reference easily understood. The reader must take this key-word not as a statement, but as the author's cue to him, so that he can call up in himself his own associations and nostalgias, and read the little poem against this background. The present collection is arranged according to the four seasons — except that it starts with the New Year. Then it quickly turns to the melting of the snow, and the first appearances of Spring. In this book the seasonal key-word is frequently omitted.

Because the poem is tiny does not mean that it is simple. A good *haiku* is apt to be not only subtle but complex, with inner meanings (often because polysyllabic words are made up of syllables which have meanings of their own; often because phrases used have literary and historical associations). Obviously it is impossible to reproduce such complex meanings in seventeen English syllables, and the present translations do not pretend to be literal or complete.

The seventeen syllables of the *haiku* are usually divided into three lines of five, seven and five. Because of the side-decorations in this edition, the longer second line here is usually doubled-up. The reader's pardon is asked for this typographic indulgence. And his attention is directed to three other collections, all the poems being different from these, available from the same publisher under the titles *Japanese Haiku*, *Cherry Blossoms*, and *Haiku Harvest*.

4

THE FOUR
SEASONS

DECORATIONS
BY MARIAN
MORTON

SPRING

SUCH A FINE FIRST DREAM...
BUT THEY LAUGHED
AT ME...THEY SAID
I HAD MADE IT UP
                    TAKUCHI

EVEN MY PLAIN WIFE...
EXQUISITE AS VISITORS
ON NEW YEAR'S MORNING
                    ISO

NEW YEAR GIFT-GIVING...
AH, BABY AT HER
BARE BREAST
REACHING TINY HANDS
                    ISSA

FIRST WIND OF THE YEAR...
THE OIL-LAMP
IN THE WASHROOM
SHUDDERS AND IS STILL
                    OEMARU

6

FELICITATIONS!
    STILL . . . I GUESS
    THIS YEAR TOO
WILL PROVE ONLY SO-SO

                    ISSA

YEAR'S FIRST CART-LOAD . . .
    CUT-OUT PAPER
    FLOWERS DECK
THE EMACIATED HORSE

                    SHIKI

FIRST DREAM OF THE YEAR . . .
    I KEPT IT
    A DARK SECRET . . .
SMILING TO MYSELF

                    SHO-U

SUN-MELTED SNOW . . .
    WITH MY STICK
    I GUIDE THIS GREAT
DANGEROUS RIVER

                    ISSA

FROM MY TINY ROOF
　　SMOOTH ... SOFT ...
　　STILL-WHITE SNOW
MELTS IN MELODY

ISSA

ICICLES AND WATER
　　OLD DIFFERENCES
　　DISSOLVED ...
DRIP DOWN TOGETHER

TEISHITSU

OLD SNOW IS MELTING ...
　　NOW THE HUTS
　　UNFREEZING TOO
FREE ALL THE CHILDREN

ISSA

A CHILDLESS HOUSEWIFE ...
　　HOW TENDERLY
　　SHE TOUCHES
LITTLE DOLLS FOR SALE

RANSETSU

8

NOW WILD GEESE RETURN...
   WHAT DRAWS THEM
   CRYING CRYING
ALL THE LONG DARK NIGHT?
           ROKA

POURING FLOODS OF RAIN...
   WON'T MOUNT FUJI
   WASH AWAY
TO A MUDDY LAKE?
           BUSON

CLEAR-COLORED STONES
   ARE VIBRATING IN
   THE BROOK-BED...
OR THE WATER IS
           SOSEKI

IN MY NEW CLOTHING
   I FEEL SO DIFFERENT
   I MUST
LOOK LIKE SOMEONE ELSE
           BASHO

OH YOU BAWDY BREEZE . . .
  THATCHER BENDING
  ON THE ROOF
I SEE THE BOTTOM!

ISSA

IMMOBILE FUJI . . .
  ALONE
  UNBLANKETED BY
MILLIONS OF NEW LEAVES

BUSON

SPRING MORNING MARVEL . . .
  LOVELY NAMELESS
  LITTLE HILL
ON A SEA OF MIST

BASHO

PASSING THE DOLL SHOP
  I PICKED UP
  THE LITTLEST ONE . . .
SUDDENLY I SMILED

BAISHITSU

THERE IN THE WATER
   COLOR OF THE
     WATER MOVES . . .
TRANSLUCENT FISHES
             RAIZAN

HAZY PONDED MOON
   AND PALE NIGHT SKY
     ARE BROKEN . . .
BUNGLING BLACK FROG
            BUSON

SILVER-SOFT RIVERSIDE . . .
   DIM SPLASH OF
     FAR-THROWN NET . . .
FISHING FOR THE MOON?
            TAIGI

PAPER-WEIGHTS PROTECT
   GAY PICTURE-BOOKS
     IN THE SHOP . . .
INQUISITIVE BREEZE
            KITO

AH-AH-AH-CHOO! THAT
   SPRING CATARRH!...
   NOW I'VE LOST SIGHT
OF MY FIRST SKYLARK

YAYU

AN APRIL SHOWER...
   SEE THAT THIRSTY
   MOUSE LAPPING
RIVER SUMIDA

ISSA

RAINFALL IN APRIL...
   TEARS FROM OUR
   WEEPING WILLOW...
PETALS FROM OUR PLUM

SHOHA

AH LITTLE WARBLER...
   THANKS-DROPPINGS
   ON MY PORCH
BECAUSE I LOVE YOU?

BASHO

12

UNDER MY TREE-ROOF
   SLANTING LINES OF
   APRIL RAIN
SEPARATE TO DROPS
             BASHO

FARMER, RAISE YOUR HEAD...
   DIRECT THIS STRANGER
   WHO WILL SMILE
AND DISAPPEAR
             BUSON

GOOD MORNING, SPARROW...
   WRITING ON MY
   CLEAN VERANDA
WITH YOUR DEWY FEET
             SHIKI

BEACH FISHERMEN GO
   BOBBING OUT...
   BEACH POPPIES STAY
BENDING WITH SEA-BREEZE
             KYORAI

EVEN THE OCEAN
    RISING AND FALLING
    ALL DAY...
SIGHING GREEN LIKE TREES
                    BUSON

I COULD NOT SEE HIM
    THAT FLUTTERING
    FLY-OFF BIRD...
BUT THE PLUM-PETALS...
                    SHIKI

GLIDING RIVER BOAT...
    RISING SKYLARKS...
    RIPPLING SOUNDS
TO OUR RIGHT AND LEFT
                    RANKO

BIRD-DROPPINGS PATTERN
    THE PURPLES AND
    THE YELLOWS OF
MY IRIS PETALS
                    BUSON

14

SHINING ON THE SEA . . .
DAZZLING SUNLIGHT
SHAKING OVER
HILLS OF CHERRY-BLOOM
BUSON

OVER THE LOW HEDGE
HONEST PLUM
DISTRIBUTES PETALS
HALF INSIDE . . . HALF OUT
CHORA

RIVERBANK PLUM-TREE . . .
DO YOUR REFLECTED
BLOSSOMS
REALLY FLOW AWAY?
BUSON

BLUE EVENING SEA . . .
FROM SPRING ISLANDS
NEAR AND FAR
NEW LIGHTS ARE SHINING
SHIKI

THE OLD MESSENGER
   PROFFERING HIS
   PLUM-BRANCH FIRST...
ONLY THEN THE LETTER
             KIKAKU

MIDNIGHT FULL OF STARS...
   DIM CHERRY-PETALS
   FLOATING ON
RICE-PADDY WATERS
             BUSON

OVER MY SHOULDER...
   MY FRIENDS WHO
   FOLLOWED ME WERE LOST
IN CLOUDS OF BLOSSOM
             CHORA

THE SEASHORE TEMPLE...
   INCOMING ROLLERS
   FLOW IN TIME
TO THE HOLY FLUTE
             BUSON

LOW-TIDE MORNING...
   THE WILLOW'S SKIRTS
   ARE TRAILED
IN STINKING MUD
           BASHO

HERE COMES MR. HORSE...
   QUICK, QUICK, OUT
   OF THE ROADWAY
HAPPY SPARROWLET
           ISSA

MOONLIGHT STILLNESS
   LIGHTS THE PETALS
   FALLING... FALLING...
ON THE SILENCED LUTE
           SHIKI

GREEN... GREEN... GREEN...
   WILLOW-LEAF THREADS
   ARE SLIDING
RIVER-RUNNING-WATER
           ONITSURA

17

CHERRY-PETAL DAYS . . .
   BIRDS WITH TWO LEGS
   GLITTER NOW
HORSES GLEAM WITH FOUR
               ONITSURA

HEAT-WAVELETS RISING . . .
   PLUM-PETALS
   DRIFTING WAVERING
DOWN ON BURNING ROCKS
                 SHIKI

COME NOW, PLAY WITH ME . . .
   FATHERLESS
   MOTHERLESS DEAR
LITTLE SPARROW-CHILD
                 ISSA

NO BOLD RAIN-CLOUD FOR
   A HUNDRED MILES
   AROUND . . . DARES
BRAVE THE PEONIES
                BUSON

IN THE CLEAR FORDING
    PALE FEET OF THE
    SILENT GIRL ...
CLOUDING MAY WATERS
                  BUSON

OPENING THIN ARMS ...
    A PINK PEONY
    BIG AS THIS!
SAID MY BITTY GIRL
                  ISSA

ULTRA-PINK PEONY...
    SILVER SIAMESE
    SOFT CAT...
GOLD-DUST BUTTERFLY...
                  BUSON

ENERGETIC ANT...
    SILHOUETTED ON
    THE STILL
SNOWFLAKE-PEONY
                  BUSON

19

IN THE YARD PLUM-TREES
    BLOSSOM ... IN
    THE BROTHEL
GIRLS ARE BUYING OBIS
                          BUSON

THAT WHITE PEONY...
    LOVER OF THE MOON
    TREMBLING
NOW AT TWILIGHT
                          GYODAI

FACING THE CANDLE
    THE PEONY ALSO
    BURNING...
MOTIONLESS AS DEATH
                          KYOROKU

THE FIRST FIREFLY...
    BUT HE GOT AWAY
    AND I ...
AIR IN MY FINGERS
                          ISSA

LISTEN, ALL YOU FLEAS . . .
YOU CAN COME ON
PILGRIMAGE, O K . . .
BUT THEN, OFF YOU GIT!
                    ISSA

BUT IF I HELD IT . . .
COULD I TOUCH THE
LIGHTNESS OF THIS
FLUTTER-BUTTERFLY?
                    BUSON

HANGING SADLY DOWN
AMID THE
MERRY-MAKERS . . .
GREEN WEEPING WILLOW
                    ROKA SHONIN

OUT OF MY WAY PLEASE
AND LET ME PLANT
MY BAMBOOS . . .
OLD BROTHER TOAD
                    CHORA

21

FOR THAT BRIEF MOMENT
   WHEN THE FIREFLY
   WENT OUT . . . O
THE LONELY DARKNESS
               HOKUSHI

NOW THIS OLD POET
   EMERGES FROM THE
   PURPLE DEPTHS
OF THE CONVOLVULUS
               CHORA

PINIONS PULSATING . . .
   YOUR MIND
   TRAVELING AFAR
BUTTERFLY DREAMER?
              CHIYO-NI

MOON-IN-THE-WATER . . .
   BROKEN-AGAIN . . .
   BROKEN-AGAIN . . .
STILL A SOLID SEAL
               CHOSU

NOW HAVING TAKEN
   WARMED WATER ...
   THE VASE WELCOMES
MY CAMELLIA
                    ONITSURA

FALLEN NOW TO EARTH
   AFTER DANCING
   JOURNEYINGS ...
KITE THAT LOST ITS SOUL
                    KUBONTA

KEEPING COMPANY
   WITH US, PIGEONS
   AND SPARROWS ...
LOW-TIDE-LOOKERS ALL
                    ISSA

WHAT, TRAVELING
   IN THE RAIN? ...
   BUT WHERE CAN HE
BE WENDING SNAILWARD?
                    ISSA

23

SUMMER

WITH MY NEW CLOTHING
   ALAS ... SPRING
   HAS BEEN BURIED
IN THAT WOODEN CHEST
               SAIKAKU

HANDS UPON THE GROUND
   OLD ARISTOCRATIC FROG
RECITES HIS POEM
              SOKAN

AS I PICKED IT UP
   TO CAGE IT ...
   THE FIREFLY
LIT MY FINGER-TIPS
              TAIGI

FLEEING THE HUNTER
   THE FIREFLY
   TOOK COVER ...
THE EVENING MOON
              RYOTA

SOFTLY FOLDED FAWN
   SHIVERS, SHAKING OFF
   THE BUTTERFLY...
AND SLEEPS AGAIN

          ISSA

THE HEAVY WAGON
   SHOOK ALL THE
   ROADSIDE ... WAKING
A SINGLE BUTTERFLY

          SHOHA

IN THE GOLDEN ROOM
   FRIGHTENED QUICK
   CALLIGRAPHY...
ESCAPING SWALLOW

          BUSON

HE WADES THE RIVER
   CARRYING THE GIRL
   AND SEE ...
CARRYING THE MOON

          SHIKI

25

FOR DELICIOUSNESS
   TRY FORDING
   THIS RIVULET...
SANDALS IN ONE HAND

BUSON

ELEGANT SINGER
   WOULD YOU FURTHER
   FAVOR US
WITH A DANCE...O FROG?

ISSA

BEFORE THE SACRED
   MOUNTAIN SHRINE
   OF KAMIJI...
MY HEAD BENT ITSELF

ISSA

RAINY AFTERNOON...
   LITTLE DAUGHTER
   YOU WILL NEVER
TEACH THAT CAT TO DANCE

ISSA

ON THE LOW-TIDE BEACH
  EVERYTHING WE STOOP
  TO PICK . . .
MOVES IN OUR FINGERS
                CHIYO-NI

FLOWER-PETAL FELL . . .
  THEN THE ROOSTER
  CROWED, AND SEE . . .
ANOTHER PETAL
                BAISHITSU

DARK THE WELL AT DAWN . . .
  RISING WITH THE
  FIRST BUCKET . . .
CAMELLIA-BLOSSOM
                KAKEI

NOW TAKE THIS FLEA:
  HE SIMPLY CANNOT
  JUMP . . . AND
I LOVE HIM FOR IT
                ISSA

THE FLOATING HERON
  PECKS AT IT
    TILL IT SHATTERS . . .
FULL-MOON-ON-WATER
ZUIRYU

FOR A COMPANION
  ON MY WALKING
    TRIP . . . PERHAPS
A LITTLE BUTTERFLY
SHIKI

AH GOOD BUDDHIST FROG . . .
  RISING TO A
    CLEARER LIGHT
BY NON-ATTACHMENT
JOSO

BATS COME OUT AT DUSK . . .
  WOMAN OVER
    THE WAY . . . WHY
DO YOU STARE AT ME?
BUSON

OVERHANGING PINE...
   ADDING ITS MITE
   OF NEEDLES
TO THE WATERFALL

          BASHO

SQUADS OF FROGS JUMPED IN
   WHEN THEY HEARD
   THE PLUNK-PLASH
OF A SINGLE FROG

          WAKYU

LITTLE SILVER FISH
   POINTING UPSTREAM
   MOVING DOWNSTREAM
IN CLEAR QUICK WATER

          SOSEKI

LOOK...THE PALACE...
   YOU CAN GLIMPSE IT
   THROUGH THAT HOLE
IN THE MOSQUITO-FOG

          ISSA

CONGRATULATIONS
  ISSA!...YOU HAVE
   SURVIVED TO FEED
THIS YEAR'S MOSQUITOES
             ISSA

IN YOUR SUMMER-ROOM...
  GARDEN AND MOUNTAIN
   GOING TOO
AS WE SLOWLY WALK
             BASHO

JUST BEYOND THE SMOKE
  OF OUR SMUDGE
   THIS EVENING...
MOSQUITO-MUSIC
             SHIRAO

DO I HEAR VOICES
  FROM FAR LANDS
   ABOVE THE CLOUDS?
O...SILLY SKYLARKS
             KYOROKU

30

SHORTEST SUMMER NIGHT...
  IN EARLY MORNING
  LAMPS STILL
BURNING ON THE BAY
                    SHIKI

MOON-IN-THE-WATER
  TURNED A WHITE
  SOMERSAULT...YES
AND WENT FLOATING OFF
                    RYOTA

EVEN FLY-SWATTING
  BY THESE BORDER
  GUARDS...O HOW
VICIOUS AND CORRECT
                    TAIGI

QUICK-PATTERING RAIN...
  CHANCE AND VANITY
  DICTATE
GAY IMPROMPTU HATS
                    OTSUYU

31

YOU HEAR THAT FAT FROG
    IN THE SEAT OF
    HONOR, SINGING
BASS?...THAT'S THE BOSS
                    ISSA

WINDY-WEB SPIDER
    WHAT IS YOUR
    SILENT SPEAKING...
YOUR UNSUNG SONG?
                    BASHO

AND EACH MORNING
    RIGHT ABOVE THIS
    LITTLE ROOF...
MY PRIVATE SKYLARK
                    JOSO

DON'T WASTE PRECIOUS TIME
    NOW, TAGGING ALONG
    WITH ME...
BROTHER BUTTERFLY
                    ISSA

EXPERIMENTING...
  I HUNG THE MOON
  ON VARIOUS
BRANCHES OF THE PINE

          HOKUSHI

SWAT SOFTLY SOFTLY
  AT THE SICK-ROOM
  FLIES...BECAUSE
I SEEK FOR SLEEP

          SHIKI

THE DEVOTED CLERK...
  NOT TO WASTE
  A JOT OF BREEZE
NAPS ON A LEDGER PILLOW

          ISSA

ON HIS GARDEN PATH
  THIS SPARROW
  SCATTERS PEBBLES...
MAN FORGOTTEN

          SHOHA

RIVER MOGAMI
   WINDING FROM
      NORTHERN MOUNTAINS
WASHES WARM SUMMER
                    SHIKI

SUMMER-NIGHT INSECTS
   FALLING BURNT AND
      DEAD ... UPON
MY POEM'S PAPER
                    SHIKI

YOU ARE JUST TOO LATE
   TO HELP ME WITH
      THE LAMP ... MY MOTH
LIGHT-EXTINGUISHER
                    ISSA

AGAIN COOLNESS COMES ...
   SILVER UNDERSIDES
      OF LEAVES
EVENING-BREEZE BLOWN
                    SHIKI

34

AFTER THAT ILLNESS
   MY LONG GAZING
     AT ROSES
WEARIED THE EYELIDS
                  SHIKI

THE NIGHT WAS HOT...
   STRIPPED TO THE WAIST
     THE SNAIL
ENJOYED THE MOONLIGHT
                  ISSA

MY SUMMER ILLNESS...
   BUT AT LAST MY LIFE
     WAS SPARED
AT THE VERY BONES
                  SHIKI

CAREFUL, CHAMPION FLEA
   AND LOOK BEFORE
     YOU LEAP...
HERE'S RIVER SUMIDA
                  ISSA

COMING FROM THE BATH...
   COOL ON HER BREASTS
     THE WARM BREEZE
OF THE VERANDA
               SHIKI

FUI! A SOUR PLUM...
   THIN EYEBROWS
     PINCHED TOGETHER
ON THE LOVELY FACE
               BUSON

HOLY NOON DUET:
   BASSO-SNORING
     PRIEST...DEVOUT
CONTRALTO-CUCKOO
               SHIKI

FARTHER IN THE GROVE
   THE LANTERN WALKS...
     NEARER NEARER
SINGS THE NIGHTINGALE
               SHIKI

WITH THE NEW CLOTHES
    REMEMBER...THE
    CROW STAYS BLACK
AND THE HERON WHITE
                    CHORA

I SCOOPED UP THE MOON
    IN MY WATER
        BUCKET...AND
SPILLED IT ON THE GRASS
                    RYUHO

MUST YOU COME TO VEX
    MY SICK EYES THAT
    STILL CAN MOVE...
BED-CRISS-CROSSING FLY?
                    SHIKI

COOLNESS ON THE BRIDGE...
    MOON, YOU AND I
    ALONE
UNRESIGNED TO SLEEP
                    KIKUSHA-NI

IN THE ENDLESS RAIN
    IS IT TURNING
    SUNWARD STILL . . .
TRUSTING HOLLYHOCK?
                        BASHO

HOT SLOW AFTERNOON . . .
    SUDDENLY THE HAND
    HAS STOPPED . . .
SLOW-FALLING FAN
                        TAIGI

IN SUMMER MOONLIGHT
    THEY GO VISITING
    THE GRAVES . . .
SAVORING THE COOL
                        ISSA

IN THE MORNING BREEZES
    CLIMBING IN A
    SINGLE LINE
GO SINGING SKYLARKS
                        RYOTA

A NEAR NIGHTINGALE ...
    BUT MY HEAD JUST
    COULDN'T FIT
THROUGH THE LATTICES
                YAHA

A SUMMER SHOWER ...
    ALONG ALL THE
    STREET, SERVANTS
SLAPPING SHUT SHUTTERS
                SHIKI

RAINFALL AND THUNDER
    BEATING ON BOARDS
    AND BLOSSOMS ...
INDISCRIMINATE
                SAMPO

RAIN-OBLITERATED ...
    THE RIVER,
    SOME ROOFS,
A BRIDGE WITHOUT A SHORE
                BASHO

39

AUTUMN

IN LANTERN-LIGHT
  MY YELLOW
  CHRYSANTHEMUMS
LOST ALL THEIR COLOR
                    BUSON

MORNING-MISTED STREET...
  WITH WHITE INK
  AN ARTIST BRUSHES
A DREAM OF PEOPLE
                    BUSON

AT NARA TEMPLE...
  FRESH-SCENTED
  CHRYSANTHEMUMS
AND ANCIENT IMAGES
                    BASHO

AN OLD TREE WAS FELLED...
  ECHOING, DARK ECHOING
THUNDER IN THE HILLS
                    MEISETSU

THE GREAT FIRE OF KANDA

HEAT-WAVES TO HEAVEN . . .
   RISING FROM THE
   RUINED HEARTS OF
THREE THOUSAND HOMES
               SHIKI

CHANTING AT THE ALTAR
   OF THE INNER
   SANCTUARY . . .
A CRICKET PRIEST
               ISSA

SAD TWILIGHT CRICKET . . .
   YES, I HAVE WASTED
   ONCE AGAIN
THOSE DAYLIGHT HOURS
               RIKEI

A SUDDEN SHOWER . . .
   TERRIFIED, LOUD
   IDIOT DUCKS
HIGH-TAILING HOME
              KIKAKU

MY MELONS THAT YOU
   STOLE LAST YEAR . . .
   THIS YEAR I PLACE
UPON YOUR GRAVE, MY SON
       OEMARU

ON THESE RAINY DAYS
   THAT OLD POET
   RYOKAN
WALLOWS IN SELF-PITY
       RYOKAN

PITIFUL . . . FEARFUL . . .
   THESE POOR SCARECROWS
   LOOK LIKE MEN
IN AUTUMN MOONLIGHT
       SHIKI

WE STAND STILL TO HEAR
   TINKLE OF FAR
   TEMPLE BELL . . .
WILLOW-LEAVES FALLING
       BASHO

42

THE EVENING BREEZES . . .
   WATER LAPPING
   LIGHTLY ON
THE HERON'S LEG-STICKS
               BUSON

THE WET KINGFISHER
   SHAKES HIS FEATHERS
   IN THE LATE
REFLECTED SUNLIGHT
               TORI

IN UNENDING RAIN
   THE HOUSE-PENT BOY
   IS FRETTING
WITH HIS BRAND-NEW KITE
             SHOHA

THE CALLING BELL
   TRAVELS THE CURLING
   MIST-WAYS . . .
AUTUMN MORNING
             BASHO

NIGHTLONG IN THE COLD
   THAT MONKEY SITS
   CONJECTURING
HOW TO CATCH THE MOON
        SHIKI

DARK UNENDING NIGHT...
   ONCE, OUTSIDE
   THE PAPER SCREEN,
A LANTERN PASSING
        SHIKI

THEY HAVE GONE ... BUT
   THEY LIT THE
   GARDEN LANTERN
OF THEIR LITTLE HOUSE
        SHIKI

ON ONE RIVERBANK
   SUNBEAMS SLANTING
   DOWN ... BUT ON
THE OTHER ... RAINDROPS
        BUSON

44

SUPPER IN AUTUMN . . .
   FLAT LIGHT THROUGH
   AN OPEN DOOR
FROM A SETTING SUN
           CHORA

SEPTEMBER SUNSHINE . . .
   THE HOVERING
   DRAGONFLY'S
SHIMMERING SHADOW
           KARO

DO I DARE DEPEND
   UPON YOU FOR
   FIRM FRIENDSHIP
DEAR MORNING-GLORY?
           BASHO

A WINDBLOWN GRASS . . .
   HOVERING MID-AIR
   IN VAIN
AN AUTUMN DRAGONFLY
           BASHO

45

NOW THE OLD SCARECROW
   LOOKS JUST LIKE
   OTHER PEOPLE...
DRENCHING AUTUMN RAIN
              SEIBI

HERE IS THE DARK TREE
   DENUDED NOW
   OF LEAFAGE...
BUT A MILLION STARS
             SHIKI

UP FROM MY ILLNESS
   I WENT TO THE
   CHRYSANTHEMUMS...
HOW COLD THEY SMELLED!
             OTSUJI

WAKING IN THE NIGHT
   I ADDED MY AUTUMN
   COUGHING
TO INSECT VOICES
             JOSO

JAGGED CANDLE-FLAME...
THE VERY SHAPE
OF AUTUMN SIFTS
THROUGH THE SHUTTERS

RAIZAN

URGING ON MY HORSE
INTO MIST-BLANKETED
WATER...
RIVER-GURGLE SOUNDS

TAIGI

WHITE CHRYSANTHEMUMS
MAKING ALL ELSE
ABOUT THEM
REFLECTED RICHES

CHORA

PEACEFULNESS...TODAY
FUJIAMA STANDS
ABOVE US
MIST-INVISIBLE

BASHO

47

SMACK-ACK...SMACK-ACK...
   MEN DRIVING
   FISH-NET STAKES
IN WHITE-FOG MORNING
          BUSON

WHITE AUTUMN MOON...
   BLACK-BRANCH
   SHADOW-PATTERNS
PRINTED ON THE MATS
          KIKAKU

EXQUISITE THE DEWY
   BRAMBLE...
   TO EVERY THORN
A SINGLE DROPLET
          BUSON

FROM THE TEMPLE STEPS
   I LIFT TO THE
   AUTUMN MOON
MY VERITABLE FACE
          BASHO

IN THIS SOLID MIST
   WHAT ARE THOSE
     PEOPLE SHOUTING
BETWEEN BOAT AND HILL?
           KITO

NIGHTS ARE GETTING COLD . . .
   NOT A SINGLE INSECT
   NOW
ATTACKS THE CANDLE
            SHIKI

HIS HAT BLOWN OFF . . .
   HOW PITILESS
   THE PELTING
STORM ON THE SCARECROW
          HAGI-JO

IN MY OWN VILLAGE
   I THINK THERE ARE
     MORE SCARECROWS LEFT
THAN OTHER PEOPLE
          CHASEI

SWALLOWS FLYING SOUTH . . .
   MY HOUSE TOO
   OF STICKS AND PAPER
ONLY A STOPPING-PLACE
           KYORAI

AFTER MOON-VIEWING
   MY COMPANIONABLE
   SHADOW
WALKED ALONG WITH ME
           SODO

AFTER THE WINDSTORM
   FORAGING FOR
   FIREWOOD . . .
THREE FIERCE OLD WOMEN
           BUSON

ROADSIDE BARLEY-STALKS
   TORN BY OUR CLUTCHING
   FINGERS . . .
AS WE SMILED FAREWELL
           BASHO

SUDDENLY CHILL FALL...
   WHY SHOULD THAT
     RAGGED FORTUNE-TELLER
LOOK SO SURPRISED?
               BUSON

ALL THE WORLD IS COLD...
   MY FISHING-LINE
    IS TREMBLING
IN THE AUTUMN WIND
              BUSON

AUTUMN BREEZES SHAKE
   THE SCARLET FLOWERS
    MY POOR CHILD
COULD NOT WAIT TO PICK
              ISSA

SEEKING IN MY HUT
   FOR UNLOCKED
    MIDNIGHT TREASURES...
A CRICKET BURGLAR
              ISSA

51

WINTER

LITTLE ORPHAN GIRL...
    EATING A LONELY DINNER
IN WINTER TWILIGHT
            SHOHAKU

IN THE WINTRY MOON
    GALES RAGING
    DOWN THE RIVER
HONE THE ROCK-EDGES
            CHORA

THE NEW-LAID GARDEN...
    ROCKS SETTLING
    IN HARMONY
IN SOFT WINTER RAIN
            SHADO

WHEN I RAISED MY HEAD...
    THERE WAS MY
    RIGID BODY
LYING BITTER COLD
            SEIBI

OVER WINTRY FIELDS
   BOLD SPARROW
   COMPANIES FLY
SCARECROW TO SCARECROW
               SAZANAMI

BATH-TUB FIREWOOD . . .
   THANKS FOR THIS
   FINAL SERVICE
FAITHFUL OLD SCARECROW
               JOSO

MY VERY BONE-ENDS
   MADE CONTACT WITH
   THE ICY QUILTS
OF DEEP DECEMBER
               BUSON

POOR THIN CRESCENT
   SHIVERING AND
   TWISTED HIGH . . .
IN THE BITTER DARK
               ISSA

SO LONELY...LOVELY...
  THE EXQUISITE
  PURE-WHITE FAN
OF THE GIRL I LOST

               BUSON

IN WINTER MOONLIGHT
  A CLEAR LOOK
  AT MY OLD HUT...
DILAPIDATED

               ISSA

BLACK CALLIGRAPHY
  OF GEESE...PALE
  PRINTED FOOTHILLS...
FOR A SEAL, FULL MOON

               BUSON

IN MY DARK WINTER
  LYING ILL ...
  AT LAST I ASK
HOW FARES MY NEIGHBOR?

               BASHO

THE OLD DOG LIES INTENT
    LISTENING . . .
    DOES HE OVERHEAR
THE BURROWING MOLES?
                    ISSA

A THOUSAND ROOF-TOPS
    A THOUSAND
    MARKET-VOICES . . .
WINTER-MORNING MIST
                    BUSON

FIRST SNOW LAST NIGHT . . .
    THERE ACROSS THE
    MORNING BAY
SUDDEN MOUNTAIN-WHITE
                    SHIKI

WHEN THE WATERPOT
    BURST THAT SILENT
    NIGHT WITH COLD . . .
MY EYES SPLIT OPEN
                    BASHO

WINTER HAVING TOUCHED
THESE FIELDS ...
THE VERY TOMTITS
PERCH ON THE SCARECROW
KIKAKU

COLD WINTER RAINFALL ...
MINGLING ALL THEIR
GLEAMING HORNS
OXEN AT THE FENCE
RANKO

SEE THE RED BERRIES ...
FALLEN LIKE LITTLE
FOOTPRINTS
ON THE GARDEN SNOW
SHIKI

WINTER-EVENING SNOW ...
THE UNCOMPLETED
BRIDGE IS ALL
AN ARCH OF WHITENESS
BASHO

56

MOONLIT SNOWFIELDS...
  HERE THE BLOODIED
  SAMURAI
CAST THEIR NOBLE LIVES
KIKAKU

MIDNIGHT WANDERER
  WALKING THROUGH
  THE SNOWY STREET...
ECHOING DOG-BARK
SHIKI

AS TO ICICLES
  I OFTEN WONDER
  WHY THEY GROW
SOME LONG...SOME SHORT
ONITSURA

IN WINTER MOONLIGHT
  FISH-NET STAKES
  CAST THEIR SHIFTING
UNEVEN SHADOWS
SHIRAO

COLDER FAR THAN SNOW...
   WINTER MOONLIGHT
   ECHOING ON
MY WHITENED HAIR

               JOSO

SO CLOSE...SO VAST...
   RATTLING WINTER
   HAILSTONES ON
MY UMBRELLA-HAT

              BASHO

LONG-WALKING LANTERN
   DISAPPEARED INTO
   SOME HOUSE...
DESOLATE WHITE HILLS

              SHIKI

SOLITARY CROW...
   COMPANIONING
   MY PROGRESS
OVER SNOWY FIELDS

              SENNA

STARING DELIGHTED
    EVEN AT WALKING
    HORSES
IN NEW MORNING SNOW
                    BASHO

BLINDING WILD SNOW
    BLOWS, WHIRLS AND
    DRIFTS ABOUT ME...
IN THIS WORLD ALONE
                    CHORA

WINTER MOONLIGHT CASTS
    COLD TREE-SHADOWS
    LONG AND STILL...
MY WARM ONE MOVING
                    SHIKI

IN THAT COLD DARKNESS
    MY HORSE STUMBLED
    SUDDENLY
JUST OUTSIDE THE HOUSE
                    BUSON

59

LOOK AT THAT STRAY CAT
   SLEEPING ... SNUG
   UNDER THE EAVES
IN THE WHISTLING SNOW
TAIGI

IN MY NEW-YEAR HEART
   I FEEL NO FURY...
   EVEN AT
THESE TRAMPLERS OF SNOW
YAYU

COFFIN AND MOURNERS
   PASSED ME WALKING
   DOWN THE STREET...
MIDNIGHT AT NEW YEAR'S
SHIKI

TO CELEBRATE NEW YEAR'S
   WE FEAST
   NEWLY-OPENED EYES ON
SNOWY FUJIAMA
SOKAN

60

DEATH-SONG:

POET NIGHTINGALE ...
   WILL I HEAR YOUR
   LATER VERSES
IN THE VALE OF DEATH?
ANON.

DEATH-SONG:

SUDDENLY YOU LIGHT
   AND AS SUDDENLY
   GO DARK ...
FELLOW-FIREFLY
CHINE-JO

DEATH-SONG:

FULL-MOON AND FLOWERS
   SOLACING MY FORTY-NINE
FOOLISH YEARS OF SONG
ISSA

DEATH-SONG:

IF THEY ASK FOR ME
   SAY: HE HAD SOME
   BUSINESS
IN ANOTHER WORLD
SOKAN